THE TEAM PHILOSOPHY OF MINISTRY

Church Growth Institute

Providing Practical Tools for Growth

P.O. Box 7000 • Forest, VA 24551

Editor: Cindy G. Spear
Designer: Carolyn R. Phelps
Editorial and Design Assistant: Tamara Johnson

TEAM Evangelism® and *TEAM Ministry*®
are registered trademarks of Church Growth Institute.

The *TEAM Philosophy of Ministry*

Contents

1185006

Preface

Rationale

Historically, churches have placed supreme emphasis on their doctrinal statement, thinking a clear statement of a church's doctrine would pave the way to successful ministry (i.e., knowledge guaranteed function). However, today's churches are realizing that effective results grow out of clearly stated goals, and goals are accomplished only when a clearly stated strategy of ministry is followed. This strategy of ministry, called a statement of ministry, must be based on a sound philosophy which grows out of Scripture and is consistent with biblical standards and objectives.

Purpose

The primary objective of Church Growth Institute (CGI) is to research, provide programs of instruction, and offer seminars for training leaders; thus being an organization for outreach, education, nurture, and renewal for the church, thereby helping individual churches reach *their own* potential. Another way of putting it is, we want to *provide practical tools for church growth.* Since rapid change will probably continue in the foreseeable future, CGI will communicate skills, knowledge, and attitudes that make it possible for leaders and laity to grow personally and vocationally, therefore equipping them to carry out their ministries.

CGI maintains links with historic Christianity, serving to uphold biblical principles and develop practical methods (systematic or orderly procedures). Our methods are adapted from eternal principles to reach specific cultures for effective ministry in our rapidly changing society; thus meeting the challenge of an information-based, technological-oriented age, yet grounded in the unchanging Word of God.

Introduction

What is the TEAM Philosophy of Ministry?

The TEAM philosophy of ministry is based on using people where they are useable. As such, it encourages everyone to use their own God-given gifts, thereby maximizing their greatest strengths while minimizing their weaknesses. It equips Christians to work together as a *team* through the local church.

A TEAM ministry church is led by the "Ephesians 4 Pastor" who is the steward of the gifts, talents, and abilities of those entrusted to his care. As stated in Ephesians 4, his responsibility is to lead his people to do the work of the ministry, not to do all the work of the ministry for them.

Simply stated, the TEAM philosophy of ministry says: God has given every member of the church a spiritual gift thereby equipping and calling them to perform the function of that gift. Therefore, the church becomes most effective and efficient when leaders utilize laity in their proper roles to do the work of the ministry.

What is a team?

The term TEAM, "people working together for the benefit of the whole," has several connotations in the TEAM philosophy of ministry.

1. *Christians teamed with Christians:* All the members of the local church work in cooperation with each other to carry out the responsibilities given to the church.

2. *Spiritual gifts teamed with spiritual gifts:* In 1 Corinthians 12, Paul uses a three-way analogy indicating that the members of the body of Christ (the church) are not only Christians but are also the various spiritual gifts possessed by those Christians. Plus, Ephesians 4:16 indicates that when gifts are fitted properly, both external (numerical) and internal (spiritual) growth will result.

3. *Laity teamed with leadership:* TEAM ministry develops a partnership between clergy and laity by recognizing that each plays a different role in the local church.

4. *The church teamed with God:* Based in 1 Corinthians 3:9, "For we are labourers together with God," the church carries out the role given to it while God fulfills the promises given to the church.

5. *Methods teamed with methods:* TEAM ministry recognizes that many different methods used over the years are valid and have a place in most churches. Many methods, although incomplete or representative of select groups, actually complement each other when used cooperatively.

6. *People teamed with methods:* TEAM ministry acknowledges that of the many different methods for reaching people for Christ, some are more suitable for some people than others.

(Adapted from the *TEAM Evangelism* Preface.)

Striving for balance

We probably recognize the greatest need for balance today in our diets. We know that to be healthy, we must eat the proper foods as well as the proper proportions of food and should balance our diets with exercise. Furthermore, we realize that improper diets can create a multitude of health problems (for instance, a vitamin D deficiency can result in a disease such as rickets or a vitamin C deficiency can cause scurvy). The possibility of some physical problems may surprise us. An extremely overweight person can actually suffer from malnutrition!

The same is true in the church. Many times churches suffer from malnutrition even when they appear on the surface to be well nurtured. Years of research reveals that there are *four* basic areas every church must emphasize to continue to grow and minister to its people. This does not mean that other areas are not important, but that if we neglect one or more of these necessary areas the church will become malnourished. And the malnourished church, just like the malnourished person, will eventually die if the problem is not corrected.

The four central areas to balance for a healthy church are:

1. *Leadership.* Leadership is not dictatorship but influence. No organization will ever rise to be greater than its leadership. The size of every church is regulated by the leadership capacity of its pastor. Leadership builds a church and makes it grow numerically while ministry meets the

physical and spiritual needs of the people, therefore maintaining growth.

2. *Bonding.* Bonding is assimilating new members into the existing church body and getting them to stick to the church. Bonding requires developing relationships and providing a discipleship program for new Christians and an orientation program for new members who come to your church by transfer. *People should be bonded to Christ and His church.* It is not enough to simply lead people to Christ. We must nurture them to become active members involved in the ministry, fellowship, education, worship, and stewardship of the local church.

3. *Lay Involvement.* Spiritual gifts are the tools for doing the work of the ministry. If we neglect the discovery and use of these tools, members will never perform as God intended. When members do not use their gifts we find an overworked staff, a burned-out pastor, and an ineffective church, and – worst of all – we find an unfulfilled laity. A team can be effective only when it is balanced through each member using his or her own gift.

4. *Evangelism.* Every church should be actively involved in evangelism. A church that does not evangelize is not only ignoring the Great Commission, it will eventually die from old age. Once a church loses its burden to reach out to its community with the Gospel it is left to minister only to itself and will become self-centered. Not only must every church have a vision for evangelism, it must also recognize two major facts affecting its workforce. 1) Every church is made up of two kinds of people, those *with* the gift of evangelism and those *without* the gift of evangelism. It is of utmost importance that any evangelistic methodology recognize and incorporate these groups accordingly. 2) Statistics prove that the most effective evangelistic outreach is through existing relationships of its members, because those with whom they have those relationships are more receptive to the church than strangers are. Only when we combine these two factors will we be able to develop an outreach program that involves the greatest amount of Christians and ultimately influence the greatest amount of lost people.

How they work together

This simple diagram shows how these four basics relate to and complement each other when addressed in the proper perspective.

Leadership is in the center because everything revolves around and is controlled by leadership. Therefore, the arrows extending from leadership indicate its influence on the success of all other areas.

Bonding is where all new members start. If they are not bonded to the local church as well as Christ, they will not stay. As a person matures in Christ, his or her next obvious step is involvement.

Involvement is what separates Christianity from religion. At this level, people are willing to invest their lives in the lives of others. Involvement provides the expression for our spiritual gifts. Note that in our diagram an arrow protrudes from involvement to leadership. This indicates the source of new leadership. As new members come to Christ and become active in the church, many will find themselves equipped to lead others.

Evangelism is the fourth, but actually not last, area. Effective evangelism starts taking place for many Christians at the beginning of their own bonding and continues through involvement, with some people (those with the gift) maintaining evangelism as the dominant area of their involvement. The process of effective evangelism continues and takes us back to where we started as it brings in more people who need to be bonded to the church.

The next four sections of this book explain in greater detail these four necessary areas of ministry. They also explain how Church Growth Institute has developed its ministry to equip church leaders with the necessary tools to lead their laity to become an effective and efficient team that literally fulfills all aspects of the Great Commission.

The Four Areas of Balance
Area One: Leadership

Surprisingly, as important as leadership is in the local church, many churches have a problem with members not trusting and respecting – therefore not following – their leaders. Most of these people, because of an experience with a leader who abused his authority, see leadership in terms of control, restrain, suppress, and dominate which are all words that better describe a dictator. However, when we look in Webster's dictionary for a description of leadership we find words like conductor, director, authority, manager, guide, principal officer, governor, initiator; one who sets the example or precedent. This definition is the view Church Growth Institute (CGI) supports. The Bible has always supported leadership. When God wanted the Israelites set free from Egyptian control He did not send angels or elect a committee but called a man, Moses, to lead His people to the promised land.

The TEAM philosophy of ministry upholds leadership as essential to lasting church growth. Leadership brings vision to an organization and Scripture says that "where there is no vision, the people perish" (Prov. 29:18). The best word to describe the TEAM ministry leader is "coach." This person oversees, directs, and leads but is still a member of the team. We call this coach the Ephesians 4 Pastor – *the steward of the gifts, talents, and abilities of the people entrusted to his care.* He influences people by being a leader, not a dictator. He knows how to work with others, how to delegate, how to give credit where credit is due, and how to get things done through others. This is the principle of work-force economics.

In addition to his training, every pastor must know three basic things in order to have a successful ministry.

1. *Who am I?* He must know his calling, his spiritual gifts, his personality, his unique strengths and weaknesses.

2. *Who are my people?* He must know their spiritual gifts, their strengths, their weaknesses, their desires, and their burdens, plus, who the leaders are among them.

3. *What is the uniqueness of the community in which my church serves?* He needs to identify cultural traits, special problems and needs, population statistics, dominant religious affiliations, and so forth.

Once the pastor knows these three things he can develop a unique strategy that will allow him to effectively and efficiently minister to his community with the help of the people God has given him to lead.

Leadership Training: CGI's unique understanding of leadership has enabled it to develop an extremely practical training technique that supports and strengthens the pastor in his leadership role as he grows and matures as a leader. Our study of leadership reveals that although successful leaders have many strengths and various factors in common, there is only one factor that *all* successful leaders have in common – *self-confidence.* Many have outstanding personalities, but not all do. Many are well educated, but many are not. Many are outgoing and personable, but some are not. But the one thing all successful people have in common is self-confidence. Therefore, at CGI we asked ourselves, "How can we provide the pastor with a tool that will help him develop confidence in himself and his church leaders?"

Before we answer that question for you, we need to explain two other basic concepts in education. We call them *academic versus practical.*

Academic deals with theoretical knowledge rather than practice. An academic approach to education basically says we teach people theories and principles that inform and allow them to make choices and apply them in life.

The theory of academic versus practical is basically *being* versus *doing.* Example: academic (being) would say, if a man studies Scripture, develops the proper attitudes, and becomes Christlike, he will *be* a good husband and father. Therefore, he will *do* the things a good husband and father does. Practical (doing) says if a man will *do* the things a good husband does, he will *be* a good husband. In other words, an academic approach develops within an individual all the characteristics he needs to become a leader while a practical approach leads him through the steps of doing what a leader does to become a leader.

Both approaches are valid. The end result is always the same. The question is, which approach is most effective for the typical, potential church leader? We at CGI believe that the practical approach is most effective for the following reason. If self-confidence is the strongest characteristic a successful person can possess, then what is necessary to develop self-confidence? Self-confidence is developed through experience, past success, and accomplishments; therefore, our approach is to offer you resources that provide practical step-by-step training to help you and your lay leadership be successful, thus instilling the self-confidence needed to become effective leaders. Continued success will give you and your lay leaders the experience and credibility necessary for developing and reinforcing self-confidence that leads to the ability to make sound leadership decisions.

CGI resources provide simple, easy-to-understand instructions and step-by-step guides that make it possible for *anyone* using these packets to be successful. These resources are similar to the old apprentice programs of the past, which offered on-the-job training. Somewhere along the line the church has drifted away from on-the-job training, to require that a person obtain years of education before he or she can be placed on the job. This lack of experience only means that the average individual has to re-learn everything he or she was taught in school. Therefore, CGI strives to create practical "on-the-job" resources for church leaders. This does not mean education is unimportant, but that theoretical experience can be even more beneficial when enhanced with proven practical tools. Our materials are designed to complement higher education, not take away from it.

CGI currently offers *TEAM Leadership* for training laity. This resource contains an 8-week course and text (*The 8 Laws of Leadership*) explaining biblical leadership qualities and helping the potential leader understand the tasks involved in leadership.

For training Sunday School and group leaders, CGI offers: *154 Steps to Revitalizing Your Sunday School and Keep Your Church Growing* (helps teachers and workers understand the principles and methods that make churches grow through the Sunday School or any small group), *Ministry Planning & Goal Setting* (a six-hour video series with guidelines and strategic principles for effective planning of short-range and long-range goals), *How to Go to Two Services* (explains the benefits of going to two services and tells how to do it), *How to Reach the Baby Boomer* (helps you understand America's largest and most influential generation and gives practical ideas for reaching them for Christ and involving them in the local church) and *The Complete Guide to Starting and Evaluating a Children's Ministry* (gives a plan of action, training and "know-how" to help children's workers develop their efforts into a real need-meeting ministry).

For the serious leader who wants in-depth leadership training in Church Growth, we offer a 20-hour video study course called *Towns on Church Growth.*

We will continually add to our selection of leadership material to help you develop leadership in the many needed areas of your church.

Area Two: Bonding

Bonding consists of actions on the part of the church and Christian individuals to get newcomers to stick to the church. If a new convert does not become part of a group within the church within two weeks of joining the church, he or she will most likely become a drop-out. Therefore, we must begin to bond people before they become active in church. To bond people, we must build good relationships.

We must realize that a three-way relationship is needed in bonding. First is the newcomers' or prospects' relationship with the individual member, second is their relationship with the church (all members), and third is their relationship to Christ. So in order to reach someone and bond them to Christ and the church, you must first win them to you, second win them to your church, and then win them to Christ.

Once relationships are developed, there are five areas in which guidance and instruction are required to keep that bond strong and keep newcomers actively involved in the church.

Basic Doctrine: A Christian must be grounded in his or her faith. It is important for a person to know why he or she is a Christian.

The Christian Family: A Christian should understand and carry out his or her proper role and responsibility in his or her own family. He or she needs to learn biblical family principles to build strong and healthy Christian homes. This, in turn, results in stronger churches.

Biblical Finances: A Christian must learn personal stewardship – how to properly manage his or her God-given resources (which includes but is not limited to finances and giving to the church). This is a major concern which is basic to the well-being of every person since everyone is required to manage money in everyday living.

Active Involvement in the Church: If a new member is not actively involved within the first three months, he or she may not become involved at all. A Christian needs to discover his or her dominant spiritual gift and understand the relationship of that gift to others in order to learn where he or she fits in the ministry and should utilize that gift as part of the church team ministering to one another. Through spiritual gifts training and realization of each one's own gifts, most members will be motivated to become involved.

Evangelism: A Christian should be taught that there is a place in evangelism for everyone and should understand the importance of actively participating in reaching others for Christ. This does not mean that everyone must be confrontational or part of the visitation program, but that each should participate in their church team by using his or her own gift and personality to stair-step people to Christ and Christian maturity.

It is crucial for every church to have an organized discipleship program. Why? Long-time Christians need to remain steadfast, be strengthened in the faith, and be fed spiritually. New Christians need to be grounded and nurtured. Both should continually strive for Christian maturity, which will be fully satisfied only when we reach heaven.

Also, new Christians are like sponges. They are ready to "soak up" every new spiritual truth they can. If your church does not provide biblical truth immediately and on an ongoing basis, you stand the chance of losing these new converts to cults and offbeat religions in their search for spiritual truth.

Therefore, Church Growth Institute recommends that every church plan and conduct basic discipleship training courses for each new member – new Christians as well as those who transfer membership from other churches. The courses should be repeated annually so that everyone receives the complete training. Although basic Bible study and topics such as self-esteem, prayer, worship, additional doctrine, and so forth are important, the five areas mentioned above are foundational and should be covered *first* to bond newcomers to the church and strengthen them in their relationship to Christ and His church.

CGI's *TEAM Ministry* and *TEAM Evangelism* both indirectly address the topic of bonding. However, *TEAM Bonding* is being created to cover bonding in more detail. *Foundational Doctrines of the Faith* teaches eight basic Bible doctrines to ground Christians in their faith and help bond them to Christ. *Gaining Personal Financial Freedom* teaches Christians biblical principles of finances and shows them how to manage their money and include the church. Other resources are currently being developed, including *The Christian Family* (a biblical guide to developing and maintaining healthy families – spiritually and emotionally.)

Area Three: Lay Involvement

Although spiritual gifts are the tools for doing the work in the ministry, the discovery and use of spiritual gifts goes far beyond a place of service. There are seven reasons why every Christian should know his or her spiritual gift. Understanding these seven reasons gives insight as to how an individual's spiritual gift relates to his or her life, church, and the lives of those around him or her.

Knowing your spiritual gift helps you understand the will of God for your life. What God has called you to do, He has gifted you to do and what He has gifted you to do, He has called you to do.

If spiritual gifts are the tools for doing the work of the ministry, and God gives you a hammer, what does He want you to do? Saw boards? No, obviously if He gives you a hammer He wants you to drive nails. Understanding this fact will enable you to make decisions as to where to serve God, how to serve God, and in many cases help you choose your occupation. But in all cases, knowing your spiritual gifts helps you set priorities for your life.

Knowing your spiritual gift helps you understand how the Holy Spirit works through you. A spiritual gift is the primary channel by which the Holy Spirit can minister *through* the believer. Spiritual gifts are God's provision for the Holy Spirit to minister to man through man.

*Knowing your spiritual gift helps you know what God has **not** called you to do.* After taking a spiritual gifts inventory, many people immediately recognize why they have had so much trouble trying to perform in a certain area of ministry. They discover they are gifted in a totally different area and find a freedom to withdraw from where they are, to get involved in the area of ministry for which God had gifted them.

Knowing your spiritual gift relieves you from serving out of "duty." If the truth were known, many of our active church workers are serving for the wrong reasons. They are doing what they are doing because the pastor asked them to, or the nominating committee honored them by electing them to this position, or if

	JANUARY	FEBRUARY	MARCH	APRIL
First Year	*TEAM Ministry* (12 weeks) *TEAM Ministry* (initial workshop) *How to Reach the Baby Boomer*			*TEAM Evangelism* (8 weeks) *TEAM Evangelism* (initial workshop) *How to Grow a Caring Church*
Second Year	*Annual Stewardship Campaign* (4 weeks) *Annual Stewardship Campaign* (4 weeks) **Basic Doctrine** (8 weeks) *TEAM Leadership*		*Spring Attendance Campaign* (4 weeks) **The Christian Family** (8 weeks) *Building a "House of Prayer"*	*TEAM Evangelism Refresher* (4 weeks)
Third Year	*Annual Stewardship Campaign* (4 weeks) *Annual Stewardship Campaign* (4 weeks) **Basic Doctrine** (8 weeks)		*Spring Attendance Campaign* (4 weeks) **The Christian Family** (8 weeks)	*TEAM Evangelism Refresher* (4 weeks)

*For an explanation of how to use this calendar, see page 20

STRATEGIC WORKING CALENDAR
for planning your strategy of church growth & ministry

MAY	JUNE	JULY	AUGUST	SE
	The Christian Steward – personal finances (8 weeks) *The Christian Steward* (initial workshop) *Night of Caring*	*Outreach Bible Study*	*The Christian Family* (8 weeks) *The Christian Steward* (initial workshop) *Living Proof*	*154 vite Su an Ch*

MAY	JUNE	JULY	AUGUST	SE
Christian ard eks) *M Bonding*		*Annual Homecoming (Beyond Homecoming – 4 weeks)* *Annual Homecoming* **The Christian Servant** (8 weeks)		*Tou er T*

MAY	JUNE	JULY	AUGUST	SF
Christian ard eks)		*Annual Homecoming* **The Christian Servant** (8 weeks)		

All Adult Sunday School Classes
Worship Services

TEMBER	OCTOBER	NOVEMBER	DECEMBER
Steps to Re-ize Your day School Keep Your rch Growing	*Fall Attendance Campaign (Friend Day – 4 weeks)* *Fall Attendance Campaign (Friend Day – 4 weeks)*	*Ministry Planning & Goal Setting*	

TEMBER	OCTOBER	NOVEMBER	DECEMBER
as on Teach-aining	*Fall Attendance Campaign (FRANtastic Days – 4 weeks)* *Fall Attendance Campaign* **The Christian Witness** *(8 weeks)*		

EMBER	OCTOBER	NOVEMBER	DECEMBER
	Second Friend Day (5 weeks) *Fall Attendance Campaign* **The Christian Witness** *(8 weeks)*	Review *Ministry Planning & Goal Setting*	

wcomers' Class
ecial Workshops (special areas of training & instruction)

they don't help in the nursery they will have to teach the fifth-grade boys. There are many reasons Christians serve in areas where they don't belong – areas that keep them busy but not fulfilled. It boils down to this: they are serving out of false duty and not God's calling.

When you use the gift God has given you, you will receive maximum fulfillment with a minimum of frustration and will become more efficient in the area in which you are gifted. No other area will bring you the same results.

Knowing your spiritual gift fills a deep inner need. The need to serve your fellow man is a need that God has put into the soul of everyone, Christian and non-Christian alike. As we use our gifts to serve in a personal ministry, we fulfill this inner need and receive more fulfillment out of life.

Knowing your spiritual gift builds unity among Christians. When you understand the characteristics of spiritual gifts you'll see how gifts influence your desires, motives, and behavior. You will see why other people don't always see things or relate to a situation the same way you do. It is all part of God's plan that different gifts complement each other.

Knowing your spiritual gift adds to your self acceptance. A young man who had just finished a study on spiritual gifts once said, "I love to teach, and I teach every chance I get. I've never done anything in the church but teach, and I really don't want to do anything but teach, nor do I intend to do anything but teach. If I go for any period of time without teaching, I get irritable and hard to get along with. I've taught for years, but you know something – for the first time in my life I don't feel guilty because I'm not *pastoring*." Many believers consider themselves unspiritual because they can't live up to the expectations of someone else. This false guilt is the greatest tool Satan uses to keep Christians from living up to their own potential.

Real winners in life are people who accept themselves. They know who they are because they have learned their strengths and weaknesses. They know their limitations and have learned to work within those boundaries. Most people do not allow themselves to be what they think they could be because *it's not what you are that holds you back, it's what you **think** you're not.*

Thus, spiritual gifts are the building blocks of the church. Many churches start with programs and try to get people to fit their needs. But many are left out because these programs don't meet their needs. A spiritual-gift-oriented church starts with its people, finds out exactly what their needs are; and designs all programs, teaching, and preaching to meet these needs. This is being people-centered rather than program-centered. We need to build with the means, not the tasks. People are motivated to action because either they have to or they want to. Spiritual gifts are the "want to" of Christian service.

To teach and motivate lay involvement, CGI currently offers *TEAM Ministry* (a spiritual gifts study to help laity understand spiritual gifts, discover their own gifts, learn how each gift works together, and find out where they best fit in ministry) and the *Spiritual Gifts Inventory* (to help Christians discover or confirm their dominant spiritual gifts).

We are now planning and writing the following nine books to help Christians develop their spiritual gifts and realize how and where to use these gifts: *How to Use the Gift of . . .*

...Evangelism(now available)   ...Teaching   ...Pastor / Shepherd
...Serving   ...Administration   ...Prophecy
...Exhortation   ...Mercy-Showing   ...Giving

Area Four: Evangelism

Matthew 28:19-20 gives us the Great Commission – to reach the unsaved with the Gospel, baptize them into the body of Christ, and teach or disciple them. This goes beyond the traditional belief of "seeking and saving" and includes nurturing Christians to maturity.

This evangelism process does not mean every Christian must be confrontational and go out knocking on doors. Those who have the gift of evangelism are able to effectively do this and should. But others should use their own spiritual gifts and personalities to build relationships and minister to others as they work as a team to network people into the church and draw them to Christ. There is a place for every person and every personality type in the evangelism process. Church Growth Institute's *TEAM Evangelism* explains how all Christians with their various gifts can work together to create an effective evangelistic outreach.

Research shows that evangelism is most effective when we deal with *existing relationships* – our friends, relatives, neighbors, coworkers, and so on. Those with whom we have developed relationships and who are most receptive and responsive to us will ultimately be more responsive to our church and our God. *TEAM Evangelism* helps you identify these potential prospects.

Although it is not necessary for Christians to attend intense evangelism training classes, we believe every Christian would benefit from personal evangelism training. There are different types of programs for different types of people. When speaking of evangelism, there are actually two groups of people: those who *have* the gift of evangelism (about 10% of church members) and those who *do not have* this gift (about 90% of church members).

People who have the gift of evangelism are outspoken individuals who are comfortable and effective in confronting people with the Gospel. They should be offered a visitation-type training program through the local church.

People who do not have the gift of evangelism still want to see others accept Christ as Saviour, but because of their own personalities or dominant spiritual gifts, they are not comfortable in confronting people one-on-one with the Gospel. These Christians should be offered a training program of how to share Christ with a friend. They do not have to be confrontational, but should be prepared to verbalize their faith when the opportunities arise. They should be witnesses – people who give testimony of what they have seen or heard. Just like in a courtroom, a witness gives testimony when he or she is put on the stand or questioned. To go one step further: If you were sitting in a courtroom and knew your testimony would make a difference in the outcome of a trial, you would feel the obligation to speak up, even if you were not called on. Sometimes as Christians we must do the same. There are a few programs available that teach how to use gifts together with evangelism in leading others to Christ.

Although you may not be the one who actually leads a person to Christ and witnesses the conversion experience, you can play a vital role in helping that person take one more step toward accepting Christ; and best of all, you only have to be yourself.

Although evangelism training is not absolutely necessary and should not be required before trying to reach others for Christ, we recommend it to every Christian – because an evangelism training course will help them be better prepared to share Christ with others and become more effective witnesses – whether or not the Christian is confrontational or meek and mild-mannered.

The following evangelistic products (giving effective strategies and organized methods for reaching people for Christ) are available from CGI: *TEAM Evangelism* (gives structure and practical application to your evangelistic outreach while providing a place in the evangelism process for both the gifted lay-evangelist and those who have other dominant gifts), *Night of Caring* (shows the do's and don'ts and explains how to do effective visitation evangelism), and *Outreach Bible Study* (a method of reaching the unchurched in their own environment – suited for people who do not have the gift of evangelism, but includes a place for those who do). We plan to offer a *TEAM Evangelism Refresher* course (a one-year follow-up) in the near future.

CGI also produces several outreach/attendance campaigns that complement evangelistic efforts. These resources include: *Friend Day, Second Friend Day, FRANtastic Days, Beyond Homecoming,* and *Sunday School Enrollment.* We will add one new campaign each year.

Planning an Effective Strategy

Every church needs to plan — to realize their purpose, set goals, and develop a strategy for reaching those goals. A growing church is one who has a vision, knows where they are going, and works toward goals. A growing church is full of members who learn together, work together, and minister together. A growing church has a committed leader who continuously grows, plans, and *leads*. To help you be an effective leader and to help your church grow spiritually and in number, Church Growth Institute (CGI) has designed many practical products and is developing many more.

We encourage you to plan a strategy to lead, teach, equip and involve current members as well as help newcomers become oriented to your church and grow as active members of the body of Christ. Several important areas of instruction should be incorporated into your ministry. CGI has many resources available to assist you in this process. By helping you build a successful ministry, we become successful in fulfilling our purpose. Although we continually develop new products and hope to some day offer everything you need for an effective and efficent ministry, we may not currently have everything you need to fit every area of ministry we have suggested. When CGI does not have the appropriate resource to fulfill your immediate needs, we recommend that you contact your local Christian bookstore or denominational publishing house to find a resource that may fill those needs. Meanwhile, we will continue to develop new and practical resources for future use.

To use our suggested strategy, first become familiar with the TEAM Philosophy of Ministry. Then establish your own statement of ministry (see Appendix). Next, help each individual identify his or her spiritual gifts. Then teach and incorporate basic strategies (*TEAM Ministry, TEAM Leadership, TEAM Bonding,* and *TEAM Evangelism*) followed by various topics derived from these main strategies. For a suggested working calendar that incorporates these strategies, see the calendar in the center of this booklet.

Our prayer is that this simple booklet will help you plan, organize, and develop a structure to lead your church to carry out the Great Commission and to reach the potential God has given your ministry.

How to Use the Planning Calendar

This section explains how to use the three-year calendar in the center of this booklet. We recommend that you detach the calendar and lay it out where you can see it as you read these instructions.

First of all, do not try to do *everything* we have laid out on our calendar, unless you have a large church with many groups of people with many different areas of interest. A small church that starts out trying to do all the recommended programs will overload everyone. In a smaller church, many members serve in several positions such as deacon, elder, usher, trustee, Sunday School teacher, etc. at the same time. There is a limited work-force and the same handful of people cannot fulfill the responsibilities they now have and be expected to constantly attend new workshops and participate in year-round campaigns. Therefore, you need to space your programs and campaigns to fit your own work-force. Review the calendar in view of your own church's membership, special needs, and possibilities, then go through and plan what you are going to do and when you are going to do it. But remember, you need to balance the four areas previously addressed in this booklet, *Leadership, Bonding, Involvement,* and *Evangelism.*

The Church Growth Institute (CGI) plan revolves around the Sunday morning services. We place heavy emphasis on Sunday morning because this is the best time to reach and involve the largest number of people. Do not make the mistake of delivering your most needed teachings on Sunday or Wednesday evenings. The people who attend these services are usually your most committed and are the ones who need it the least. In other words, the ones who need it the most only attend on Sunday morning.

We have set forth a plan for three dominant areas: *Sunday School (or Bible study time), worship service,* and the *newcomers class,* plus *special workshops* to be held on Saturdays or during week-long evening sessions. The following explains each area in detail.

ADULT SUNDAY SCHOOL *(represented in red on the calendar).* Use your Sunday School, Bible study time, training hour, or other regularly scheduled classes (for our purpose we will define this time as Sunday School) to disciple your adults and introduce the TEAM Philosophy of Ministry to your entire church the first year. Instead of assuming your regular members will automatically "fall in," you should start off with a basic program that will introduce and bond them to the TEAM Philosophy of Ministry. *TEAM Ministry* teaches our basic philosophy of using people where they are useable. *TEAM Evangelism* continues that philosophy, but gets everyone involved in outreach at their own level. One year following your initial teaching of *TEAM Evangelism,* you should teach the *TEAM Evangelism Refresher* course, then reteach it yearly. It reemphasizes the importance of evangelism, the importance of spiritual gifts and reinforces the TEAM philosophy of ministry.

NEWCOMERS' CLASS *(represented in blue on the calendar).* The object of teaching *TEAM Ministry* and *TEAM Evangelism* first is to get people (members and newcomers) grounded in the philosophy to bond them to Christ and your church. You will want to teach *TEAM Ministry, TEAM Evangelism,* the Christian steward and the Christian family to every member, new and old, throughout your entire adult Sunday School system the first year. Starting the second year, teach these five basics of bonding – basic doctrine, the Christian family, the Christian steward, the Christian servant (*TEAM Ministry*), and the Christian witness (*TEAM Evangelism*) – to every newcomer, whether they join your church by baptism, statement of faith, or letter. The newcomer may have been a Christian for 20 years or more, but you still want to encourage him or her to go through this foundational orientation course, because what you are teaching bonds them to *your church's* philosophy of ministry. You may cover areas with which they are not familiar or in which they have no real background. This process bonds the newcomer to your church as well as your philosophy of ministry.

NOTE: The reason the five areas are stressed so heavily this first year is because we want to ground the new or growing Christian in these major areas of his or her life. The five programs together should, at the end of the first year, have the individual biblically grounded in his or her faith (know why he or she is a Christian and be able to defend his or her faith), grounded in his or her family (know and understand his or her God-given role), grounded in his or her personal finances (understand the biblical principles for managing money and material resources), attending church on a regular basis, actively involved in the work of the ministry, and, last but not least, able to influence those he or she cares about the most for Christ. Let's face it, these areas are where we all live, and being grounded in them – in our everyday life – will make us much more receptive and make learning easier in the many areas in which you still need to teach.

If you regularly have six or more adult newcomers, initiate an ongoing newcomers class that meets every Sunday during the Sunday School hour. Every year you should start the series (the five orientation classes) over, so every new member has the opportunity to study the entire course. It may be best not to start a newcomer in the middle of any one of the subjects, because it would be nearly a year before they get back to the first part. If you have only one or two new members every month or so, put someone in charge of working with newcomers on an individual basis. Let the newcomers study at their own pace. In this case, you will need to provide the newcomers with a textbook and a workbook and lead them through this material. Some people will finish the course in a couple of weeks; others may take months. The person in charge should encourage them to use the workbook and should contact them regularly to see if they have any questions. This (the workbook and questions) adds accountability to the program. Presently CGI offers *Foundational Doctrines of the Faith* and *Gaining Personal Financial Freedom* that may be used in the bonding process. We are developing other materials for this area. Meanwhile, if you are at the point where you need a specific topic or product CGI does not offer, please check with your local Christian bookstore, a Christian publisher, or your denominational headquarters for materials to address your particular need. CGI will eventually have what you need and you will probably want to look at our products as they are released, but do not wait on us if you need them now.

The first year will be very demanding because your Sunday School time is dominated by these new orientation courses and the year ends with a Sunday School campaign. Afterwards you can get back to regular teaching. Meanwhile, continue to teach and preach your regular messages in the worship service other than when certain suggested sermons are preached along with specific campaigns. Always remember to provide a *balanced* teaching and preaching ministry, covering various subjects that are needed.

At this point many people ask: *Why do I need to teach these materials to the whole church? Why can't I just set them up as elective classes?* Because if you adopt this philosophy of ministry for your church, all your people need to be keyed in on it. They need to know what they believe in order to serve and represent your ministry well. You need their support. Otherwise, if your existing members are not familiar with your philosophy and your new members are learning and accepting the philosophy, problems will rise. The existing members may not understand or see things the way you do. You need to spend the first year orienting and getting all your members going in the same direction. Then the following years those people can assist you in keeping the church moving in the right direction. They will serve as the leaders to carry out the church's objectives.

We also recommend that when you introduce a new adult-oriented program to your church, you not only teach it initially in Sunday School, but start off by having an all-day Saturday workshop for your leaders. Many of these people are the teachers who will teach the material to others in the future. Others may teach children or have other responsibilities during Sunday School and will *never* get more than bits and pieces here and there. Therefore, the Saturday workshop benefits and is necessary to reach and train your current leaders. Send personal invitations and phone calls to get all your leaders to the introduction workshops.

WORSHIP SERVICES *(represented in green on the calendar).* For the most part CGI recommends that you conduct your worship services as usual, except during attendance and stewardship campaigns. However, after special days (attendance campaigns, etc.) which draw visitors, we recommend that you start a new series of sermons. Give the series a title that relates to practical living and announce it the day you have all the visitors. This will help create interest and persuade many visitors to return.

Attendance campaigns. We suggest that you have at least one attendance campaign per year, but no more than two. Never have three, because by doing so, all the planning and work involved would keep your entire church so busy that other necessary areas of ministry would be neglected. Plus, if you load up with too many campaigns, and do them right, you'll end up teaching the campaign themes and nothing else. Many churches have an annual Homecoming which ends up being an attendance campaign. Homecoming is an opportunity for more than a social event. It should be used as an evangelistic outreach also. Although Homecomings are sometimes in the summer, most are held in early fall.

Make sure the high day of your attendance campaign does not become the end in itself. All the work leading up to the high day is for the purpose of gathering prospects. The real work of an attendance campaign comes after the high day when the follow-up begins. All CGI campaigns have built-in follow-up. When plan-

ning, be sure to allow time after your campaign to do adequate fo
low-up. This is the only way you will get results.

If you have never held an attendance campaign, your fir
should be *Friend Day*. Of all the campaigns on the market, *Frien
Day* has proven to get the best results with the least amount of r
sistance. Do not overuse any attendance campaign, even if it pr
duces excellent results. For variety and better results, alterna
and use at least two different ones. Some of CGI's attendance cal
paigns take four weeks of worship services while others take up
seven weeks (plus follow-up). For greater results, run your cai
paign (attendance or stewardship) in both the worship service al
Sunday School. Plus, reinforce the theme through announcemen
and updates in all services. An attendance campaign that becom
only a casual event seldom returns your investment of time al
money. When all areas for your public ministry are saturated wil
the theme, your harvest will be much greater than your i
vestment. For your benefit, CGI produces one new attendan
campaign per year. We currently offer: *Friend Day, Second Frien
Day, FRANtastic Days, Beyond Homecoming,* and *Sunday Scho
Enrollment.*

Stewardship campaigns. We recommend that you have a stev
ardship campaign every year. We have found that when church
teach total life stewardship in this format, their members not on
are more successful with personal money management, but a
also more faithful in their stewardship to the local church. Als
pastors do not need to "preach" on financial needs all the time
experience results. (Never *preach* giving, *teach* stewardship.) Son
churches have a stewardship campaign at the end of their fisc
year. Many have one in November before Christmas and before tl
beginning of the stewardship year in January. Others choose
have one during December because Christmas puts people in
more generous spirit and they are more likely to make a commi
ment or pledge during that period. Still others have the
stewardship campaign at the beginning of a New Year when ever
one is making resolutions and starting the year off. Schedule yo
stewardship emphasis whenever you believe it is best for your ov
church.

Stewardship programs currently available from CGI ar
*Where Your Treasure Is..., God Is Able, Tithing Is Christian, I
vesting in the Harvest,* and *Our Family Giving to God's Family.*

Again, we recommend that you do not use the same campaig

wo years straight. As with the attendance campaigns, CGI plans o release one new stewardship campaign per year.

PECIAL **WORKSHOPS** *(represented in purple on the calendar)*. Special workshops may be scheduled as often as once a month, but you lo not need to have them that often. We have scheduled them at andom and suggest that you set up these programs to be taught at n all-day Saturday meeting or a week-long meeting – maybe 2 to hours a night, Monday through Thursday, with a break and reeshment half-way through each meeting or schedule sandwiches nd chips for a light meal before or after the meetings. For the nost part these workshops can be scheduled at any time of year. he only exception would be that some workshops should follow ertain other programs (for example, *Night of Caring, Outreach ible Study,* and *Living Proof* should follow *TEAM Evangelism* ince they are evangelism-related and complement the teaching of *EAM Evangelism. 154 Steps to Revitalizing Your Sunday School nd Keep Your Church Growing* is aimed at Sunday School teachrs, therefore, we recommend that you teach it as you begin a new unday School season.) All CGI programs give you step-by-step intructions on how to conduct a workshop or extended class, plus ow to promote and attract the greatest number of people to your vorkshop.

Leadership-oriented *Ministry Planning & Goal Setting* is best sed at the end of a year – probably in November before the holday season – as you are planning for the following year. Every two ears you should review it to instruct new people in leadership poitions and refresh those who have been through it before.

Other special resources now available include *How to Grow a aring Church, Towns on Teacher Training, How to Build a Prayng Church, How to Start or Evaluate a Small Group Ministry, The omplete Guide to Developing and Evaluating a Children's Minstry,* and *TEAM Leadership.*

Other tools. CGI offers a variety of manuals and resources eared toward church leaders to simplify the responsibilities reerved for leadership. These materials are not designed for teachng your laypeople. In this category, we currently offer: *Public Reations for the Local Church, Stewardship Letters, How to Develop Pastoral Compensation Plan, How to Go to Two Services, The omplete Guidebook to Church Hiring, How to Handle Conflict, Iow to Supervise Church Staff and Volunteers,* and *Evangelism ools for the 90s. How to Reach the Baby Boomer* is a similar type of program, but provides a section to be taught to laypeople to help them understand this generation and how to minister to them and involve them in local church ministry.

Questions

Do I have to start on January 1? No. You can start at any time during the year. However, some workshops or campaigns need to be in the order we suggest, because they complement and should follow specific programs or end at a certain time. For example, to get the best results, a fall attendance campaign should always be held with "time-change" Sunday being the high attendance day. A spring attendance campaign's high attendance day should be Palm Sunday. The reason is that it is naturally easy to get newcomers to return the following Sunday – Easter. Never let your high day fall on a holiday; no one will be available to do the necessary follow-up.

How can we afford these programs? You may wonder, "We're just a small church. How can we afford all these programs?" You may need to purchase a couple and gradually work up as you are able or you may want to take up a special offering for the materials. If you need $150, you could ask for 15 people to give $10 each or 30 people to give $5 each. You may even have a person with the gift of giving in your congregation who would pay half or all of the cost. If you plan to teach the materials in Sunday School, you could ask class members to purchase their own textbooks and workbooks. This is a common practice in many churches. Perhaps the church would purchase the necessary materials for those who truly cannot afford to do so themselves. Then you may be able to work some, if not all, of the material into your next year's budget. After all, CGI resources are an *investment* because they can be used over and over again to the benefit of your church and the advancement of God's work.

Most CGI resources are reproducible and allow unlimited copying for use within your own church. This allows you to cut your expenses considerably when actually conducting a campaign or course. Our only restriction is that you cannot sell your reproductions or pass them to another church. Each church must purchase their own resource packets.

Now, it's time to get out your own calendar and plan your strategy for growing a strong and healthy church.

Appendix
Sample Statement of Ministry

(You may edit or reproduce this as is for use within your church.)

Ministry Goals

1. To build a caring atmosphere and a team spirit within the body of Christ so each member will be accepted into the team, enabling him or her to grow physically, emotionally, and spiritually, and to help other members grow as he or she grows, resulting in team members ministering to each other.

2. To make the church an island in a hostile world where each Christian can come for worship, strength, identification, learning, equipping, strength, and fellowship.

3. To develop an effective outreach ministry, involving and utilizing the gifts and personalities of every member to stair-step those people they care about into the body of Christ. To offer a place of service to meet needs and fit the various spiritual gifts within the church – without ever forcing anyone into a mold they do not fit.

Ministry Purpose (Eph. 4)

1. To provide balance in the church by correlating programs and creating the structure needed for overall growth and ministry potential.

2. To help all believers discover and use their God-given spiritual gifts so each one, according to their strength, is ministering to others according to their needs; with the objective that the total body will grow and each individual will become spiritually mature. (We do not want to violate the integrity of any by manipulating them into a position for which they are unqualified and uncomfortable, but will help all fulfill their dreams and potential through the church by offering places of service and utilizing each Christian where they best fit in ministry.)

3. To communicate leadership attitudes and skills to every
    leader and layperson so all will grow into greater lead-
    ership positions of ministry within the church and within
    their personal life.

4. To prepare each member to carry out the ministry of the
    church by providing them tools to accomplish these
    tasks.

5. To minister in and through small groups, thus bonding
    each believer to a small group, so that both the in-
    dividual and church are strengthened. (The church grows
    numerically and spiritually by adding groups for min-
    istry, thus fulfilling the strategy of the body growing by
    the division of cells.)

6. To help all believers in their task of evangelism, reaching
    their friends, neighbors, and relatives through existing
    relationships, sharing Christ with those beyond their cir-
    cle of acquaintances, and becoming part of a team evan-
    gelistic outreach, thereby ministering to and reaching
    others for Christ through networking and bonding them
    to the church and ultimately to Christ.